Lake Erie

Great Lakes of North America

Harry Beckett

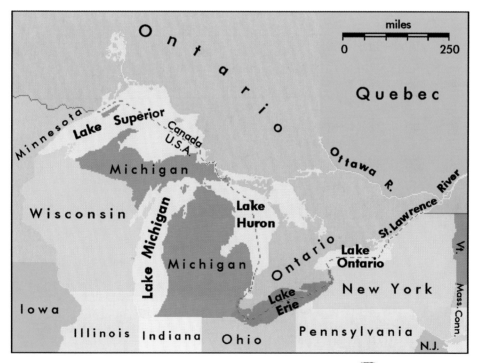

The Rourke Corporation, Inc.
Vero Beach, Florida 32964

PHOTO CREDITS:
Photographs by kind permission of: Geovisual, Waterloo, Ontario; National Archives of Canada; Buffalo Convention and Visitors Center; Cleveland Convention and Visitors Center; Fathom Five National Marine Park Tobermory, Ontario; Michigan Tourist Board; Erie Historical Society; Maps by J. David Knox

CREATIVE SERVICES:
East Coast Studios, Merritt Island, Florida

EDITORIAL SERVICES:
Susan Albury

Library of Congress Cataloging-in-Publication Data

Beckett, Harry, 1936-
     Lake Erie / by Harry Beckett.
         p. cm. — (Great Lakes of North America)
     Includes bibliographical references and index.
     Summary: Discusses Lake Erie's geography, history, early inhabitants, important events, economy, and more.
         ISBN 0-86593-527-0
     1. Erie, Lake Juvenile literature. [1. Erie, Lake.] I. Title. II. Series:
Beckett, Harry, 1936- Great Lakes of North America.
F555.B43 1999
977.1'2—dc21
                                                                99-14508
                                                                CIP

Printed in the USA

TABLE OF CONTENTS

12/7/99 RPG 17.45

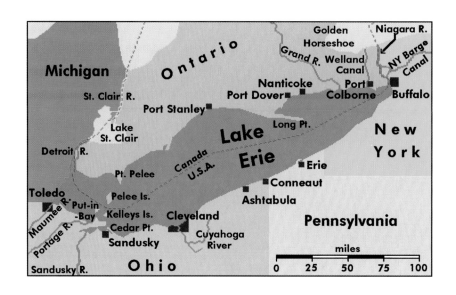

FACTS AND FIGURES FOR LAKE ERIE

Length	241 miles	388 kilometers
Width	57 miles	92 kilometers
Average depth	62 feet	19 meters
Maximum depth	210 feet	64 meters
Volume	116 cubic miles	484 cubic kilometers
Water surface area	9,910 sq. miles	25,700 sq. kilometers
Shoreline (inc. islands)	871 miles	1,402 kilometers
Area of basin	30,140 sq. miles	78,000 sq. kilometers
Height above sea level	569 feet	173 meters
Retention time*	2.6 years	

* The average time that it takes for a molecule of water to enter and leave the lake.

ABOUT LAKE ERIE

Lake Erie is further south than the other Great Lakes, and as far south as northern California. It has New York State, Pennsylvania, and Ohio from east to west along its southern shore and Michigan at its western end. The province of Ontario borders its northern shore. It is the fourth largest of the five lakes and contains the least amount of water, but it is still the eleventh largest lake in the world.

Most of its water comes from Lake Huron through the Saint Clair River, Lake Saint Clair and the Detroit River system. Other **feeder** (FEE dur) rivers are the Maumee, Portage, Cuyahoga, and Sandusky, all in Ohio, and the Grand in Ontario. Erie is the shallowest of the lakes and the water stays in it for only 2.6 years before flowing through the Niagara River and the Welland Canal into Lake Ontario. All of its islands—the biggest is Pelée Island—are at the western end.

Because the lake is very shallow, the water warms up quickly in the summer and freezes early in winter. People have built cottages along the shore to enjoy the warm summer water and the great beaches. The land around the lake is a low, **fertile** (FUR tul) plain made up of **silt** (SILT) and clay left behind by ice-age glaciers, with rocky areas at the east and west ends. It erodes easily, and the silt in the lake can drift, blocking the natural bays and harbors. Many have to be **dredged** (DREJD) and protected by piers and breakwaters. Two fingers of drifted sand, Long Point and Point Pelée, jut far out into the lake from the Ontario shore.

Point Pelée, looking north

Fierce storms from the west sometimes pile up the water at the eastern end of the lake. This is called setup. It can be several feet higher at that end than at the other. Sometimes a single heavy wave, called a seiche wave, rushes along the lake like a tidal wave.

Wetland has been preserved at Maumee Bay near Toledo.

NATIVE PEOPLES AND EARLY EXPLORERS

The lake is named after a little-known native people, the Erie, who lived on the south shore between modern-day Buffalo and Sandusky. The French only had one meeting with them, and what they knew about them came from the Huron. They were farmers and lived in **fortified** (FOR tuh fide) villages. Though they had no firearms, they were brave warriors and resisted the Iroquois fiercely before they were scattered or adopted by other nations.

North of the lake was a closely related nation that the French called Neutral because they did not take sides in the wars between the Iroquois and the Huron. But they were not neutral toward other nations. They were warlike and invaded the territory of tribes such as the Potawatami in Lower Michigan. They lived in longhouses in fortified villages built on high ground and lived from farming (corn, beans, squash, sunflowers, and tobacco), with some hunting and fishing. They, too, were finally destroyed by the Iroquois.

Some believe that the French explorer Étienne Brulé (1615) was the first European to visit Lake Erie, others believe that it was the French Canadian Louis Jolliet (1669). In 1679, the French explorer René-Robert Cavelier de La Salle built his ship, the *Griffon*, on the Niagara River between the falls and Lake Erie. French missionary Louis Hennepin's sketch shows La Salle, Hennepin, and the master shipbuilder talking in the foreground. Nearby, a workman is shaping a beam with an **adze** (ADZ), while others are **caulking** (KAHK ing) the timbers. In the background, the blacksmith is threatening a Seneca with a hot iron bar.

The building of the Griffon beside the Niagara River.

The British defeated the French in the struggle for control of the lake and developed trade along it. British Loyalists arrived on the north shore some years before the south shore was opened up around 1796.

The Griffon, *the first ship on Lake Erie*

TOWNS AND CITIES

The city and suburbs of Greater Cleveland (population 505,616) stretch 90 miles (144 kilometers) along the lakeshore and 25 miles (40 kilometers) inland. It lies mostly on a 66-foot (20-meter) high plain, but Cleveland's Public Square, an area of monuments and tall buildings, is 659 feet (201 meters) above the lake. The Cuyahoga River Valley, an entertainment area called the Flats, is half a mile wide and divides the East Side from the West Side. About eighty ethnic groups with about sixty languages live in Cleveland. It has a large parks system with a big zoo and an aquarium.

13

On University Circle, there are museums of art, history, natural history, and health. Cleveland has the Rock and Roll Hall of Fame, as well as major league baseball, football, and basketball.

Toledo (population 332,943), named for Toledo, Spain, began as a French fur-trading post at the mouth of the Maumee River. Next, it passed into British control, then to the United States. After the War of 1812, it grew quickly and both Michigan and Ohio fought over it. This is called the "Toledo War." The U.S. government gave Toledo to Ohio, and Michigan received the Upper Michigan Peninsula. It is an excellent harbor on the Saint Lawrence Waterway, with rail, road, and pipeline links to large industrial areas.

Buffalo (population 328,123), the second largest city in New York, stands at the western end of the N.Y. State Barge Canal, at the mouths of the Buffalo and Niagara Rivers. Buffalo (bison) were not native to the area, so the name probably comes from *beau fleuve*, French for "beautiful river." *Walk-on-the-Water* (1818), the first steamship on the upper Great Lakes, was built in Buffalo.

The entrance to Hope Memorial Bridge, Cleveland

Immigrants (IM uh grunts) from many countries have come to this friendly city. Buffalo was home to two U.S. presidents, Grover Cleveland and Millard Fillmore. A third, William McKinley, was assassinated there. It has an important art gallery, orchestras, and museums, as well as major league football and hockey.

Buffalo, with Lake Erie in the background

WORKING AROUND THE LAKE

Lake Erie, with its excellent ports, is an important link on the Saint Lawrence Waterway and the New York State Barge Canal. Limestone and iron ore from Lake Superior are unloaded at Cleveland, Ashtabula, Conneaut, and Buffalo. Coal arrives at Toledo and Sandusky. These are the raw materials of the steel industries of Pennsylvania and Ohio. The steel is used in Lake Erie cities to produce ships, automobiles, and airplanes.

A network of pipelines meets on the south shore of Lake Erie. It brings petroleum and gas that local industries turn into oil and gasoline, chemicals and plastics. Toledo is called the "glass capital of the world." Other cargoes arriving at Sandusky and Buffalo (a large flour-milling city) include grain from the West as well as lumber and meat.

All these cities export their own products through their ports. They also ship goods onward that have arrived on their excellent road and rail systems. Buffalo is an important gateway for U.S. exports to the Golden Horseshoe of Ontario.

The ports on the Canadian shore, such as Port Dover and Port Stanley, are mostly small. Nanticoke has a large steel manufacturing plant, an oil refinery, and one of the world's largest coal-burning electricity-generating stations. Port Colborne is the point of entry to the Welland Canal. The Niagara River has been **harnessed** (HAHR nust) to produce plenty of clean electricity.

There are many farms on the fertile land around Lake Erie.

Agriculture is important around the lake. The soil is fertile and the climate is moderate. Heavy industry polluted the lake. The fishing industry, which almost disappeared because of that, has begun to grow again, and now yields 220,462 tons (20,000 tonnes) per year.

A laker passes through the Welland Canal. Note the railway, another means of transport.

DISASTERS AND MYSTERIES

On September 10, 1813, as he lay at anchor in Put-in-Bay, Oliver Hazard Perry received word that a British fleet was approaching. When he ordered his ships to set sail, his situation was bad. The wind was light and against him. As the fleets closed slowly, the wind dropped and then sprang up again, this time in Perry's favor. As the ships maneuvered to bring their guns to bear, Perry hoisted his flag which bore the words, "Don't give up the ship." The U.S. flagship *Lawrence* was so badly damaged in the battle that Perry transferred to the *Niagara,* which was lagging behind the fighting.

The fleets fought until many ships were too damaged to sail. The British admiral, Barclay, was badly wounded and the British flagship *Detroit* became entangled with the *Queen Charlotte*. When the British were forced to surrender at the Battle of Put-in-Bay, they lost control of Lake Erie and U.S. territory that it could no longer defend. During the battle, two thirds of the *Lawrence*'s crew and one third of the sailors on the *Detroit* and the *Queen Charlotte* were killed or wounded.

Erie is a difficult lake for larger vessels to navigate because of its shallowness. During storms, the waters pile up quickly into dangerous waves. Also, ships cannot sail in a straight line because of the shoals and land spits, and there is always a danger of collisions. But it was not the lake that caused one of the greatest disasters.

Battle of Put-in-Bay

The side-wheel steamer *Erie* was headed for Chicago with over two hundred Swiss and German immigrants aboard when there was a great explosion. Fire roared through the ship. She burned quickly to the waterline and sank. Between 100 and 175 people perished. When the wreck was raised, $200,000 in melted silver and gold was found on board. The reason for the fire? It is thought that painters had left cans of turpentine on the deck above the boilers.

The Burning of the Steamship Erie

INTERESTING PLACES

Called one of "America's Undiscovered Family Escapes," Kelleys Island is a short ferry trip from Sandusky past the Marblehead lighthouse. It still has only a hundred full-time inhabitants, and it has more deer than people. Visitors have been coming to this beautiful, unspoiled island for over a century. There are hiking trails, a sandy beach, a campground, boat-launching facilities, and excellent year-round fishing. The center of activity is the Village, with its quaint shops and restaurants and the Lake Erie Toy Museum.

There is history, too, on Kelleys Island. Glacial Grooves State Park contains the world's largest evidence of retreating ice-age glaciers. Native American etchings on Inscription Rock show scenes of earlier aboriginal life.

The island has its own winery surrounded by vineyards and country gardens. Visitors can rent a bicycle or a golf cart to get around the island.

The Perry Victory Monument is at Put-in-Bay, just across the water on South Bass Island. Nearby Cedar Point has the largest ride park in the world with 67 rides and 13 roller coasters, including the world's tallest, fastest, and steepest. The park has hotels, a water park, and a beach.

Cedar Point, Sandusky

Point Pelée National Park is at the end of a long sand spit that juts away from the Ontario shore. It is a protected area of rich **deciduous** (duh SID juh wus) woodland and marshland. From the boardwalks that wander through the wetland it is possible to see reptiles and amphibians not seen anywhere else in Canada. This is a popular spot for birdwatching. Two major bird migration routes cross at Pelée and observers have spotted over one hundred species in one day. It is also a stopping off place for monarch butterflies as they make their long journey south.

A family at the Naval and Military Park in Buffalo

GLOSSARY

adze (ADZ) — tool used for shaping logs and heavy pieces of wood

caulk (KAHK) — fill cracks to keep out water (or cold air)

deciduous (duh SID juh wus) — has leaves which fall off in winter

dredge (DREJ) — clean out or deepen a channel or harbor

feeder (FEE dur) — a river or stream which adds to another river or body of water

fertile (FUR tul) — able to produce good crops

fortified (FOR tuh fide) — made stronger or more secure

harness (HAHR nus) — control the force of something for your own use

immigrants (IM uh grunts) — people who move into a country from another

silt (SILT) — fine grains (of sand or dirt) on the bottom of a body of water

"Butterflies" resting before they set off on their long flight south

INDEX

FURTHER READING

You can find out more about the Great Lakes with these helpful books and web sites:
- Robert MacDonald. *The Uncharted Nations,* The Ballantrae Foundation, Alberta.
- Thomas and Robert Malcomson. *The Battle for Lake Erie,* Vanwell Pub. Ltd. St
- Catharines, Ontario
- Arthur J Ray. *I Have Lived Here Since the World Began,* Key Porter Books
- Pierre Berton. *The Great Lakes,* Stoddart
- F. Stonehouse. *Went Missing,* Avery Studios, Michigan
- Chambers of Commerce of Buffalo, Sandusky, Toledo, Cleveland

- www.great.lakes.net
- d.umn.edu/seagr
- sparky.nce.usace.army.mil
- www.epa.gov/glnpo
- www.rootsweb.com/~oherie/1/pic2.html
- sg.ohio-state.edu
- www.bbaillod.cgi.execpc.com/www.board/html
- www.ohiotourism.com
- Quizzes on the Lakes: www.hcbe.edu.on.ca/coll/lakes.htm
- www.hcbe.edu.on.ca/coll/lakes.htm